HISTORIES

Very best wishes to
Agnes from
   Anne
 & Alex

By the same authors

Anne Born:
Lighting Effects
Figures for Landscape
Slant as an Open Door
Seeing Through

Alex Smith:
The Appetites of Morning, the Languor of Afternoons
Kayserling

HISTORIES

Anne Born
and
Alex Smith

UNIVERSITY OF SALZBURG
SALZBURG - OXFORD - PORTLAND

First published in 1998 at **Salzburg University**

EDITORS: WOLFGANG GÖRTSCHACHER & JAMES HOGG

ISBN 3-7052-0159-X

INSTITUT FÜR ANGLISTIK UND AMERIKANISTIK
UNIVERSITÄT SALZBURG
A-5020 SALZBURG
AUSTRIA

© Anne Born & Alex Smith

Front cover: Fort Charles, Salcombe (Photograph Anne Born)

Anne Born and Alex Smith are hereby identified as the authors of this work in accordance with Section 77 of the Copyright, Designs and Patents Act 1988.

Distributed by
    Drake International Services
    Market House, Market Place,
    Deddington OXFORD OX15 0SF
    England
    Phone 01869 338240
    Fax N°: 01869 338310

Distributed in the U.S.A. by
    International Specialised Book Services Inc.
    5804 NE Hassalo Street
    Portland
    Oregon 97213-3644
    Phone 503.287.3093
    Fax: 503.280.8832

Acknowledgements

Thanks are due to the editors of the following magazines in which some of the poems first appeared: *Bound Spiral, HQ Poetry Magazine, Links, Orbis, Other Poetry, Otter, Seam, Smiths Knoll, The Tyndale Society Journal, Westwords.*

'Saxon Studies' was a runner up in the Yorkshire Open Poetry Competition.

HISTORIES

1	At Life	1AD	AB1
2	The Blessing	1AD	AS1
3	Warrior Horse	1AD	AS4
4	The Ending of Sacrifice	3/400	AS2
5	Occupation Force	750	AB2
6	Naming	750	AS3
7	Dazzled I	850	AB3
	Dazzled II	850	AB3
8	Saxon Studies	7-991	AS5
9	Gytha's Sherford	1068	AB4
10	Roosticocks	1069	AB5
11	William of Falaise at Dartington	1086	AB6
12	Romanesque	1098	AS6
13	A Surgeon's Tale	1199	AB1
14	Eleanor of Aquitaine	1203	AB9
15	Into the Dark	1238	AB11
16	Ox carts at the ford	1250	AB7
17	Miasma	1349	AB8
18	Miasma - the response	1349	AS7
19	A problem for Paston	1448	AS9
20	A Lenten Antiphon	1453	AS8
21	Mistress Simnel considers...	1471	AB12
22	Robert Whitingham, at Owlpen	1471	AB13
23	Margaret of Anjou at Owlpen	1471	AB14
24	Privy to the King	1483	AB15
25	William Caxton ponders...	1485	AS16
26	The Greyhound of Henry VII	1487	AS10
27	The Ruminations of Mr. Perkin Warbeck	1497	AS14
28	Wm. Tyndale considers his task	1525	AS17
29	Henry's Reformation	1535	AS11
30	Fountains Abbey	1539	AS12
31	'Drowned like Rattens'	1545	AB17
32	Banbury Cross	1577	AS18
33	Matthew Godwin	1586	AB16
34	Zeal-of-the-Land Busy	c.1600	AS13
35	The Inventory of Edward Cookes	1620	AB25
36	Civil Disorder	1646	AS15
37	Feeding the Siege	1646	AB18
38	Brixham Redlanding 1688	1688	AB19
39	View from the Coffee House	1690	AS19
40	Witchcrazed	1710	AB20
41	Hogarth's Progress	1750	AB21
42	Pleasure Box	1764	AB23
43	The King, the Poet and the Whore	1767	AB22
44	The Age of Reason	1767	AS23

45	William Cowper leaves John Newton's house	1774	AS20
46	John Cookes of Kennington walks...	1780	AB24
47	After the Stirling Ranges...	1827	AB26
48	From the Unpublished Diary of Syms Covington	1833	AB27
49	The Engineer	c.1850	AS22
50	A Victorian Christmas Card	1854/5	AS24
51	Little Wife	1861	AS21
52	Brothers	1890	AB28
53	1915	1915	AB29
54	Sepia	1902/09	AS25
55	Peacock House	1926	AB34
56	1943	1943	AB30
57	1990	1990	AB31
58	William's Century	1997	AS26
59	1997	1997	AB32
60	At Life - 2000AD	2000	AB33

INTRODUCTION

In 1995, two poets with a passion for the subject decided to make a sweep of English history. It would be regarded through the eyes of both real and invented characters, on whom we eavesdropped through a time-travelling spy hole. The method offers views of each century or period, showing events experienced chiefly from the sidelines.

As we wrote the poems they crossed the country between Devonshire and Essex, our domiciles, and were discussed by letter and telephone. The pace set itself and did not need to succumb to late 20th century fever. Our aim was to depict the life of people against the landscaped background of their times in the plain language of poetry, and we left them free to determine the form and mode of their expression.

Anne Born
Alex Smith

At Life
1 A.D.

Green when I walk from the shelter.
I stand here, my leg is healed.
Green washes dark from my eyes
and the smell! Sweet as honey
you've climbed and climbed a tree for.
A bird starts up in the leaves.

I walk to the top of the hill,
green drapes around me.
Eyes as clear as a single day
give me distance over rolling
land that is ocean
yet with its waves at peace.

In those spaces the crowned trees
are centuries. Free of roots
I move and watch their way,
see each leaf grow and fall,
each bird at life, and our hours
filled with all we sing of.

The Blessing

nature's bonfire burns on

In those spaces was a glimpse of Eden.
Some talked of a return but I could not
be sure of anything like possession.
I was content that leaves should fall and rot.

Seasons were gentle, years benign:
a tumbling cornucopia at life,
or Heraclitean wheel, that burning sign
of harmony restored amid our strife.

We had no need of Eden or its myth -
the swelling hills confirmed our innocence -
guilt was a monster to be wrestled with,
to tame the mind's own dark inheritance.

I stood among the ordered hills: eyes clear
scanned distant plains, blue as Titian's groves;
our freedom rested in that lack of fear,
a freedom to pursue our doubtful loves.

IAD

Warrior Horse

whitely
freely
chalk came through
to meet astonished hands
the martial head
gradually taking shape

white horse
white warrior....

I clamber up the ridge
and stand before it
awestruck

its long back-line
strikes across the downs
commands our vision
of landscape
stuns the valley to silence

rider of rain and wind
breathing cold air and turf
it stares uneasily
from its hewn eye

could it curse us
with that stare
bridle
at its chain of chalk?

did we free its spirit
or tie it down ?

perpetual rider of the hill
white rider of the storm
lord of all weather

warrior spirit of our land

Uffington

IAD

The Ending of Sacrifice

We listened to dark voices:
    'No peace, no crops,
    no redbrown pots
    or hub of hearth flame
    without a death;
    no gentle scented hand
    on the shoulder,
    no quiet restraint,
    no peace at home
    without sacrifice'.
              Thus, the voice
of the terrible god.

A female child,
chosen and bedecked
with may - thorn's blossom -
is stretched
on the Centre Stone.
She is the entrance
to the New Year,
our rite of passage
to abundance,
high point of festival.
We pray to the god
that our sacrifice
be accepted,
will propitiate
the dark voices.

Singing is followed
by dance: countless pairs
of feet drum the ground,
countless bodies whirl
in frenzy, our flares
amaze the night.
            Dark voices:
carried by wind,
wound into the air
we breathe, darkening
the colour of words
on the tongue -
        who can deny them?
For the god had spoken:
        'Remove her heart'.

Year after year
we buried them
with honour,
along the pathway
towards the end of land,
from Morvah to Madron
where poets are honoured,
greening the land,
sleeping their innocent sleep.

But we had failed to see
how each year follows
an inevitable course,
when the sun becomes
a red ball veiled in mist
and the ground is frost-hard;
a time of dearth and hunger,
ice and cruellest cold
over the land.

Stillness
under the hand of death.

We crouched low and were still:
no roots or fiery drink,
no visions, *no voices*:
we were in the cold
of our mind
mourning dead children
gone from our lives.

And suddenly we knew:
the dark voices spoke
our own words; we ourselves
were the 'terrible god'.

300/400

Occupation Force

She dreams the valley in innocence
as it once was
at the start of her trek into sounds
that tuned into words.

Axe barked at wood
as dogs sent their signal at evening
then gave the word over to nightjars
and a minatory owl.

Her mother's scent and hands
that made everything possible
were more there than the redbrown pots
at the hub of the hearthflame.

And her mother's eyes when the Saxons
came to change her even seasons,
and the stranger's reek -
his strut of possession -
after her father had gone
turning to raise a hand
before he walked over the crest
to sink slowly,
foot knee heart and head
gone from the stunned valley.

750

Naming

Thames - the peaceful river-
cold silver in dusk
winding through dense thicket

or glancing darkly
beneath storm clouds,
a mirror
for the angry sky.

We ride
through quiet fields,
Brigid and I, laughing,
carefree, at peace.

Her black hair flows
in the freshening breeze
so like a river
I could name it:
Avon or Isis -
Brigid's raven hair
that entwines me at night.

She will bear
our children:
strong riding sons
or daughters
that will laugh like her.

How shall we name them,
our children?
After rivers and flowers?
Columbine?

And will she die,
bearing children?
Perhaps.

Then will I be
man-mother,
slow, ageing swiftly,
drifting through dry days;

or leave them
with a carer,
hunt alone. Such
bitter thoughts.
And her laughter
will return
to haunt me,
full of pain.

Where then
would I hide my face?

750

Dazzled I

Walked the cliff track, feedsack shouldered,
muffled in fur and frost, warmed
by motion and the low sunlight of Christmas.

Its slant dazzle plundered my sight
and shone the smooth slates of the path.
First the lookout point at the wood's end,
on to the crags above the bay,
down to the stream at valley level
and up to the pasture field's old walls.

That was my route.
But before the high rocks
locked out the sun
a stronger gold moved
into the glare that held me.

Blinking I walked straight into it.
Struck something. A body,
hard as a breastplate.
Above it a head helmeted
with the sun's colour,
a hood of hair.

No breath to scream at first.
He spoke, in a tongue
alien as himself,
giving his name,
gripping my arm. 'Harald.'
'Edith.'

Dazzled II

Then I was walking with him
                    into the sun
our arms touched when we moved
                    out of step
each time a lightning-strike
                    from the sky
and my feet hardly earthed
                    stepped into flight.

Rounding the corner at
                    the highest point
I looked down into Starehole Valley
                    astounded.
Our pasture slopes with their old
                    stone walls
moved with new sheep among
                    our flock
smoke rose by the stream from
                    a dozen fires.

The sun had forsaken the valley.
                    Purple shadow
darkened my dazzled eyes
                    stopped my breath.
'They will come,' my father had said,
                    'in their time.'
I'd not listened. Again I heard his voice.

They were here. In this place I held
                    as mine.
Safe as my mother, our hearth,
                    our land.
And I walked with him here,
                    invader,
into their stronghold. I
                    whose forebears

had sailed here too, arriving
                    in their time
in what they called history
                    and I
knew as my lifelight, there
                    in our walls
our church, its stone tower holding
                    our safety.

850

Saxon Studies

Bretwalda*

        i

The 'stern rebuke' harried him
from across the grey ocean,
from English-born bishops
working in Germany,
Boniface among them.

So what.
He could imagine
the mutton grease oozing
along their wizened chaps
as they spoke.

And what is to be discovered
in a word? 'Ruthless'
to his accusers,
but 'fearless' in his own heart.

        ii

If not Christ then Woden
who was, after all,
his ancestor and would serve
just as well. So,

he would continue
to wear his enemies' scalps
and nail their flayed skins
to church doors.

        iii

And what
was a fine woman for
if not another wife?
Let them answer that.

He observed a similar movement
of muscle in the face:
his own satisfied grin   ** Ethelbald*
and their revolted grimace.   *Ruler of Britain*

The Smaller Kingdoms

    i

Fearful of signs and omens
    they played at kings.
Rump companions crowded
    an ungenerous hall,
huddled against the weather.

Intense loyalty extolled
    and made a fetish:
private gestures became overt
    while teeth ground on treachery,
all eye contact avoided.

    ii

A dangerous admixture,
    piety grafted
onto barbarism: soldiers
    of Christ slicing through flesh
or patiently hearing bones crack.

Brooding silence and tension
    freeze the atmosphere;
not a place to bring a lover,
    some dark-haired girl
fresh from her mother's hearth.

700/900

Battle-fragment

....Maldon no Iliad but Essex-man
hacked to pieces in the marsh.
Such fidelity to soil.

And was he conscious of history's tide,
or the telling contingencies
of awaited dawn? Pumped high
by adrenalin's urgencies
he had no such regard, nor could he heed
the bittern's soulful boom
or cornflower deep among the reeds.

*Defeat of Bryhtnoth,
Ealdorman of Essex, 991.*

Gytha's Sherford

Gytha knew this rise, built
a small house for prayer

sited on quietus.
Earl Godwin's wife

mother to king and queen
lady of sorrows

I hope its beauty
brought you solace.

Some old stones
used in the rebuild

may have seen your face.
A blueslate flagstone

felt your tread.
The yellow bedstraw

we noticed by the gate
moved at your passing,

in this small place unaware
of fratricide at Stamfordbridge,

slaughter at Senlac,
William at Exeter's gate.

Your last flight from England
moved towards unknown ending,

but Sherford's clear stream runs on,
and after a thousand years

pellitory-at-the-wall
with ferns and mosses

still roots in the rough mortar
below the tower's west window.

1068

Roosticocks

Cuthwin came running from the shore
screaming: 'Danes coming! Arm!'
ãlfric seized his club,
yelled: 'Bar the door!'
and ran, tall as a tree.
Minutes after, felled...

They scythed down our men,
drank our ale, and roaring fell on us.
Laughed at our struggles, killed our children,
used us, and slumped.
I pulled myself from under him
to see my son lie quiet, asleep?
Then I saw blood slide beneath his head.

The other women's faces were stone like mine.
None wept.
We whispered fast and found our weapons,
waited for first light.
Then signalled, all
called like the rooster, shrieking
Roosticocks!
We fell harder on them
than they had surged on us,
and used our knives well.

I ãdwen dressed my ãlfric for the grave,
his face slashed by a pagan sword,
back broken as my heart.
I ãdwen carried my son ãthwold
close to the breasts that had nurtured him.
We buried them
beside the burnt-out church,
the priest's black shell
stretched on the black altar.

Then piled the killers' carcases on the Ham
pyred wood, straw, every burnable thing.
We set a light that turned the sea to blaze
while they spat their fat at us.

We howled them down.
But when the flames fell, turned away, quenched.
As one, we walked to the ruins,
held each other, wept.   *1069*

William of Falaise at Dartington

Twenty years from home
in this rich wilderness
given by Duke William.
A score of manors
to hold in a doubtful clasp.
Rich enough, but each grain
has to be dragged from them,
churls, serfs, heavy-fleshed hags.
Hate flicks like lightning
in this draughty hall.
I hear tales of Beornwynn, lady of roses,
beautiful magic. Her voice echoes
in the owl, the nightingale.
Omens shift the air.
Dead rats are laid at my door,
a child once. I trod on it,
heavy after drink. When it gets bad
I go to Judhel's round keep in Totnes,
hear home voices. Too much water
divides me from Normandy,
too much in this black river
threatens. It claims a heart,
they say, each year.
I dream of drownings,
the bloated fact that's always mine,
even in a child. Turned-away eyes
still pierce, clutch like brambles.
I think the conquered are strongest.

1086

Romanesque

In exchange
for the ecclesia's demands
this cavernous dark,
rouge et noir,
a housing fit and proper
for Cuthbert's bones.

Heaving rollers like dark thunder:
ropes strain at the heft and drag
of sandstone blocks cut ready
for massive piers.

Rearing like a rock face
through needle rain
and northern mist -
the townspeople cower
as though beneath ramparts,
scowling, superstitious,
remembering their dead.

Scandal:
a Sheila-na-gig
is discovered carved
in one of the transepts.

The tower is measured
and declared to be square;
more climbing scaffolds are fetched
to stem the loss of life.

Hours spent
positioning the hoist -
the masons arguing endlessly
over safety of access
to the tribune.

Forty years and quick work.

Sparrows twitter, trapped
in the gloom:
'And each one
remembered before God'
says the unctuous satin-clad reeve
before making his exit.

The iron fist in a velvet glove:
beneath the silk-embroidered
fleur-de-lis a close-knit byrnie
that can crush another man's ribs,
extinguish his air pipes
against a pillar.

The hubris of prince bishops
is enough: debt and honour
to that other Kingdom
so easily absorbed
by the temporal power.

'Fill the coffers!'
Places sold
for the consecration
will pay for more relics.

The end is achieved:
'slow, solemn rhythms' match
chill penitential chants of lent.

Durham, 1098

A Surgeon's Tale
After Chalus

Rain fell when they called me to the king.
I knew he had gone unarmoured
close to the wall, eager to take the tower
before dark. Now dark had entered him,
its arrow deep in his neck, the shaft
broken as he tried to draw out the head.
Darkness spread. I called for torches.

Their light blurred too as I set out
my instruments. The king did not moan.
His teeth were strong to stand such clenching.
And his fists. I've extracted arrows
by the dozen from most parts
of men's anatomy.

This one was too close to a vertebra
to cut at ease. I dug into flesh and fat,
the quick of a man under my hand
that had to deal so hard. I sweated, swore,
gouged more. Lack of light failed me,
and I, his doctor, took a king's life.

Next day the wound turned black.
After our victory Richard sent
for Pierre Basile the crossbowman
who had shot for revenge
on father's and brothers' deaths.
He offered to take torture.

But the king told him, voice a thread,
'I forgive you my death' and freed him.
Richard died at dayclose
in Miles his chaplain's arms.

Poor body: target for the killer,
giver of life, and in the end fouled clay.

I have seen many wounds, too many.
Given more pain than cure despite
the physician's creed: to cure sometimes,
relieve often, comfort always.
I have not cured King Richard,
nor could that coeur de lion
stop arrow or rot.
                                                        1199

Eleanor of Aquitaine Remembers

How Louis wept when I,
his queen of courtly love,
left him to racked memories.

Conveniently
my new young husband's kingdom
and mine united bodies and land.
Eight children carried through
three score and ten months
of my eight decades,
five riding sons, three feisty daughters,
took me long enough
and travels took me further.

I did not see it, but the stories
that would divert the centuries told
how Henry when enraged
by sons and archbishop Becket
would hurl himself to the floor
and chomp the rushes.
People backturned, embarrassed.
I thought
of peaceful reedbeds and the labour
to cut them, snick of stem,
suck of water around boots,
birdsong,
and frugal fare in a bare hut.

And then a clatter of oxcarts, swish
of whip and rushes scattering
as men scattered under Henry's sword.
Some years I kept to Aquitaine my home
and lived as muse to troubadours
truth-finders whose honour was doubted
by thickpate soldiers in their butchers' songs.

Green grow the rushes O
and men are all cut down.

I had given life and love
to a king's children while the king
took lives and lands till those children
turned on him
and left him to die at Chinon

His servant came to me and made me weep.
I had shared passion and work with the king,
even suffered imprisonment at Winchester
(a comfortable confinement, like my others)
to ease his politics,
but mourned that at the end he knew defeat
by kin and death. Carried conquered
to the Abbey at Font,
his chosen place
for the rest I hope he finds.

Our son Richard,
cub's heart fleshed out to lion's,
my whole concern throughout a decade more.
Until again at Fontévrault
three years ago I stood by Richard's bier,
as widow mourned the son
I cherished best
(in parenthood the hardest task
is loving equally).
And now they lie in stone,
beauty that outlasts soft rags of flesh...

It is winter in Aquitaine.
Trees and my bones are bared, they shudder.

1203

Into the Dark
Two merchants are making for home
in midwinter 1238
under cloud that bears down on their backs
and the rich bolts of cloth
weighting the pack-asses' backs in crucks.

Their way is oiled in mud, the sides
fenced with furze. They slouch in a doze.
Then the slow rhythm breaks as a man
surges out of the brush,
his cudgel cracks into their skulls
again and again and Blackdown
jolts with their cries. Gone dusk

night throws a pall of cold stillness
over two humps on the ground.
A fox with green headlights
volplanes without sound
to nose out the scene.

Come day people are busy:
finding the bodies, tracing the goods and the killer.
At the eyre next year he is charged
and found guilty: 'So he is hanged.'
As simple as that, a stopped breath
in the records of history, his chattels
'Worth 4 marks,'
himself a drop of four words into death -

1238

Ox Carts at the Ford

Thames - he had heard the name
as he walked this new land
after the rack of a sea voyage,
trudged tracks over chalk, slept
on the earth with one companion brother.

At the ford in a hill-rimmed bowl
of green, he sits near the river,
sees fritillaries lean to the winds.
Here is level land, easy to clear.
He rests under an oak. A blackbird intones.

Beside him a tower builds,
gold stone like his sunlit south,
another nearby, roofs, windows.
He hears plainsong rise above blackbird's.
Books arrive on ox carts

for libraries. 6000000 books
to stack above and below
a quadrangle's ground, windows lit
with candlepower that circles
each letter, page and hand.

Later a clatter of plates
clashes with bells that call
from chapels to study and prayer.
Then a feral chorus yells
to jolt him out of the scene,

an uglier sound of dispute,
like philosopher's discourse
or raging divinity schools.
Splatters of hate and blood
stain sandstone halls.

The shout of the future fades.
His foot comes to rest on a stone
that blooms yellow. The river
lulls through his dream, flows like learning,
runs on away and out of his time.

1250

Miasma

Your Grace, I write while I can,
hoping to hear from you in health.
Our village is struck and only God
knows if we have a future. The Lord

chastises us. He sent us sickness
in a stranger's coat left behind
in the carrier's cart, given to Joan
the woodcutter's wife, against rain.

She fell into fever, great boils bloomed
upon her, and before she died
came to our convent, breathed
poison into our air, we cannot be saved.

That polluted breath spread in the wind,
fell out upon all who walked under the sky.
Joan's daughter, the poor maysed maid,
dropped lifeless in the street. Her mother

saw the cloud over Black Tor
swelling with great mushroom heads,
heard roaring under and overground,
and enormous rats blackened the earth.

Few are escaped. My sisters
sicken daily at their work. No comfort
except hope that's hard to hold.
Expect to see no more of me in this world.

The shroud of cloud has me enfurled,
I pray hands will live to bury us
away from cold tainted air, turfed
warm by our brothers in Christ.

1349

Miasma - a bishop's response

My Dear Sister-
I was greatly saddened to receive your letter.
You are indeed under siege with the sickness
of black boils attacking you from all sides.
For this reason visits are precluded -
we must not allow the influence of this pestilence
to infect our company. I know that I have
your perfect understanding in this matter.
As for the woodcutter's wife, do not mourn
overlong: the poor are always with us
and she can easily be replaced.
Your writing at all to me is something awkward
as it touches my authority
over your Order, but as you have no abbess
at present you may be sure of my support.
I have, I admit, doubts about your cloud.
Take care to avoid hallucination:
visions have bedevilled the Church for too long
(women being afflicted in this way especially).
Take the teachings of Mother Church to heart
and follow all necessary precautions:
plague altars must be visible night and day
and closed so as to show the Christ lying dead
in His tomb; offer prayers to Saint Sebastian,
patron of plague victims, at every office;
finally, bury the dead quickly in lime pits .
Your tone suggests you may be wanting in faith
but that must be a matter for the new abbess
when appointed. This letter will be brought
to you by Roger, the idiot-boy
who may be trusted to deliver it.
Bend his inclinations so that
he is minded to stay with you.
We must avoid danger of infection.
The blesséd Trinity ever have you
in his keeping.
     Yours in faith,
      William,
      + Winchester.

1349

A Problem for Paston

O westron wind...

Purchasing the Gresham property
from Thomas Chaucer, son of Geoffrey,

a poet sometimes at court, old William Paston
was extended but satisfied.

But following his death there arose
one Moleyns, recently made Lord, who laid his claim:

the reversion of the title by option
notwithstanding its expiry.

Dry and complex, like all legal business.
Cronies mustered to make a weak claim

appear the stronger: Heydon (lawyer)
and Tuddenham (Sir Thomas) creatures both

of the duke of Suffolk (recently decapitated)
pursued their cause, not through the courts,

but by force, seizing the manor, and this
the seventeenth day of February,

the year of Our Lord, 1448.
Such hard hearts found at the heart of winter.

when will thou blow?

So John Paston appealed to Moleyns himself.
One can but try the Christian act.

Meanwhile, John's wife Margaret held the fort
against John Wymondham, ally of Heydon:

Right worshipful husband...
as the parson of Oxnead was saying mass,

just before the Elevation, James Gloys
our serving-man came homeward with his hat

upon his head. 'Uncover thy head!'
demands Wymondham and Gloys

replied, 'So I will, for thou!'.
Thus did Wymondham draw his dagger

saying 'Wilt thou, knave?' and at that Gloys turned
and drew his dagger, but defending himself,

flew to my mother's place. Then did Wymondham
and his man Hawes throw stones and drove Gloys back,

calling him thief and saying they would kill him.
They threw a stone, big as a farthing loaf

into my mother's hall. Then Hawes ran to fetch
a spear and sword and they caused an affray.

The small rain down can rain.

Then Wymondham called my mother and myself
strong whores and said that all the Paston family

were... but I am so weary of this business...
that a Christian woman should suffer so.

He continued with much strong language
as I will tell you later. So we went home

but Hawes saw Gloys standing in the street
and with a two-handed sword assaulted Gloys

again, and Thomas, my mother's man. He let fly
a blow at Thomas and grazed his hand with the sword.

For this later assault, the parson of Oxnead
saw it all and will vouch for it.

So, on my mother's advice, I am sending Gloys
to be with you for a time, for some peace of mind.

In good faith, I would not have
such trouble again for forty pounds.

Christ, if my love were in my arms...

Meanwhile, Paston made no cause with Moleyns
all summer, the spring being frittered away.

And I in my bed again!   *1448*

A Lenten Antiphon

Walter Frye   *(d.1474/75?)*
Johannes Ockeghem *(c.1420 - c.1495)*
John Dunstable   *(c.1390 - 1453)*

    i
A spring awakening:
the ditches flowing
and melt water running
in the blue light.

Bleached clear by winter,
fronds and filigree
of the scoured landscape
burgeon, break
into green spears.

Sonorous choristers
stop the heart,
lift the soul
among celestial spheres.

    ii
Ash in the mouth:
the distilled purity
of the solo treble
is not wounded by love.

Each careful glance betrays
cold depths of hunger:
their supplications prick
the flesh, revive
the smouldering fires of lust.

The saints are veiled for shame.

1453

Mistress Simnel Considers the Pretensions of Kingship

His hands are still, who always swept away
the sawdust at day's end.
The Mayor's table's unfinished,
his servants hammer our door.
Oxford stifles this summer, air is scarce.

Air. My son needs air.
Stuck in the king's kitchen
scraping greasy pans, scrubbing boards.

Priest Richard Symonds took my son.
For their own ends plotters
worked the young clay of him,
told him he should be king;
and said he is related to great men.
Priest. Man of God? Man of men,
seeking unjust rewards.
He has his reward: a prison cell
for what life may be left him.

And Lambert. Crowned in Dublin
with Our Lady's golden circlet.
Crowned in another sense,
knocked circling in air unwinged,
an Icarus bound to fall.

The Yorkists lost at Stoke,
Lambert was taken prisoner.
Dusted into a ghost, he was,
the messenger, wearied out.
I went to the workshop,
told my husband. His tools stay still,
saw halfway through a plank.

And now today I hear
Lambert has leave to wing his way
out of the scullery, into the sphere of birds.
A falconer! Keeper of the king's hawks.
King Edward, in his own gilded cage,
sees the lad was born to fly.

Now Lambert cares for hunting birds,
hoodwinks them, binds them in jesses,
feels their airy dream of freedom,
their drop to keeper and chain.   *1471*

Robert Whitingham, at Owlpen, on 3rd May, 1471
The Eve of the Battle of Tewkesbury

One thing we have agreed on:
she will not fight tomorrow.
Not that I doubt her mettle.
God knows our strengths are tempered,
both tried in fires of battle, hardship, loss,
confinement. Caged at Alnwick Castle in '63
all that could cheer me was the thought
of her, Queen Margaret.
It helped to drive off battle-ghosts,
ease pain of frostbitten wounds in Towton snow,
the bitter slaughter of thousands
whose blood ran hot before.

*

Sweet Jesus, this is a place of peace,
how can death walk in such a garden -
and I feel a dark deeper than this spring night
threatens. Tewkesbury.
The name plagues me.

An owl predicts, bats fly, a dog
in the stableyard howls.

My Lady, can you sleep? You never say,
only your weariness shows in the gaze
you turn on Edward, your hope and only one.
No gaze of shewolf or tigress,
your strength is drawn
from your royalty and need to nurture
a dreaming husband and a child in danger.

You have ridden further than any other lady
since your marriage day, when, seasickness past,
and your hair a straight black waterfall
you took Henry for worse, and set out
on the lifelong campaign to counter
his weakness with your sinew, your laughter.

1471

Margaret of Anjou at Owlpen

Scent visits me. The closed window
can't keep it out. Honeysuckle -
le chèvrefeuille, climbs

as it did in Anjou.
Moi aussi, I battle upward.
I have fallen in this warring land.
Tomorrow I must not fall.

I shall not wear armour, ride into combat.
Nor sit on a throne, that is half lost.
A seat is comfortless
without a husband recrowned.

I shall fight well enough, waiting,
dreading. The shewolf, tigress
they saw in me knows the deeps
of fear. For Edward,
my son and king to be.

Arrays of swords approach.
All my limbs are pierced,
even my womb that quickened him.

Owl, be bird, not harbinger.
Tomorrow I am tigress again
even though I shall not see him ride
into the bloody field,
dragged from the shelter
of this gracious house
as from my body.

1471

Privy to the King

Richard hunches on his close-stool.
Outside the door, Tyrell's on guard.
'When every man of them's a fool
who'll rid me of those little bastards?'

Tyrell holds his nose. Under the door
seeps the reek of kingship.
Richard strains and grunts. No more,
complains his gut. Tyrell's quip

on royal hogshit stays unheard.
Not Richard's words. Tyrell knows
the king's constipated till his word
takes princes' breath for his bowels to flow.

Duty done, Richard emerges
and Tyrell bows, checks his own breath.
Decision fouls the air and purges
king's guilt of innocent death.

1483

William Caxton ponders on his friend Malory, lately fallen into a sad condition

He uncovered enchanted landscapes, bright
encampments, replete with their baptised dead;
Arthur was blazoned abroad in perfumed May,
his banners unfurled, flaunting in the breeze.

Malory: winnower of injured chivalries,
master-teller of sorrowful pageants...
how I wept at 'the dolorous death
and departing out of this world of them all'.

His words touch the heart of our fidelities,
call to mind the soul's proper condition;
welcome as bees in early summer,
they shall be preserved for our children's sake.

But now he lies stinking of the prison house
accused of manslaughter and rape
amid blue bread, rats and ordure.
O what renown for such brave enterprise!

How should I abjure my oath of friendship,
abandon him to calumny and ill fame?
As one belonging to the Round Table
I extend my hand: his words shall be pressed.

1485

The Greyhound of Henry VII

stone-whitened
to a gloved softness

gently rampant
in heraldic abeyance

in the coolness
of its over-smooth form

the suede underbelly ripe
for the griffin's rip and tear

    ...

*King's College Chapel,
Cambridge*

1487

The Ruminations of Mr. Perkin Warbeck

An inheritance of blood: all their battles'
mesh and mire unseating reason.

This dizzy kingdom with its thrones of sand
entices boys to play the parts of men -

we smother the more troublesome.
A man's property is hardly his own life.

Even the innocent thrush chills the flesh,
spreads fear like ice along the spine

while virtue spins topsy-turvy,
helter-skelter in this world.

Oh, Cornwall, that mad peninsula
of jagged granite, early primrose....

and still they gape, clinging to their billhooks
with no more wit about them than the beasts

they keep. The shadows of the Tower encroach
and darkly cloud my everywhere mind.

I fear that I am loosening, amazed.
Fear like ice... I shudder but may rally yet -

what man is there that dare deny
that I am King Richard the Fourth?

1497

William Tyndale Considers His Task

In the beginning God, the word,
the free property of all men.

How dusty, besmirched
and covered a thing
it has become, its glory
hidden from men's eyes.
We lack
our rightful epiphany.

An overdressed age -
domed hat, ruff and doublet
conceal the man, separate
him from virtue.

Great *Jehovah* is in the frost,
speaking to the bone -
iced diamond of the will.

Seasons turn, time runs away
with the melting snow,
the quicksilver brook
glints in the February sun.
Spring, reminder of age, accuses -
the mind must now bend to the task,
unto that which is left undone.

The spirit is willing,
but the flesh is weak -

so many recant at the sight
of their instruments -

   "Shew them, that their minds
   may turn from heresy."

The powers that be
would tear the tongue from my head.

Christ, jewel of the new covenant,
spills rubies against
the retreating snow,
sheds his five wounds.

God shall be spoken:
'a boy that driveth the plough
shall know more of scripture'
than these Pharisees.

My neck upon it.

1525

Henry's Reformation

He flays about
in the echo-chamber
of his anger,
righteous and over-confident.

Courtiers, half hidden
in ruff, excuse themselves,
withdraw early and,
as Osric, bow too low.

Courtesans advance
with caution, lest boldness
burst the blister
of his rage.

1535

Fountains Abbey

Nature reclaims history:
pigeons weave a network
of shadow across the walls,
grass flows through the nave
and crossing, caps
the broken column.
The centuries retreat,
belie with silence
passions that gripped
these bare ruined choirs.
Now autumn sunlight
brings beneficence,
bestows gold upon
the untried day.

1539

'Drowned like Rattens'
The Mary Rose sinks off Portsmouth

As the wind struck
  while we were going about
I was in the forecastle
  mending a broken rail.

The Frenchies were close
  and we set sail quick
as King Henry watched from the shore.
  I dropped tools, grabbed the rail.

She started to list
  and the water came in.
I heard it above the shouts
  that turned into scream after yell.

Blown like a leaf
  from that 'flower of all ships'
I struck out for shore
  away from the hull as she fell.

Turned for one look
  she was over and down
and the calls were too few
  but I sighted the shore.

Reached it at last
  not far from the king:
'Oh my gentlemen
  Oh my gallant men' - then he swore.

I looked all around
  and saw no one.
But floating safely ashore
  the square of our backgammon board.

And a viol swam music
  to the waves' shocked lament
for my hundreds of mates
  in the sea god's hoard.

'Drowned like rattens.' All, all.
  But not our scaly-tailed crew.
As I stood there shaking and safe
  the black pack of them made landfall.

1545

Banbury Cross

(Mary Herbert, Countess of Pembroke)

In the Spring of the yeare, when the Stallions were to leape the Mares, they were to be brought before such a part of the house, where she had a vidette (a hole to peepe out at) to looke on them and please herselfe with their Sport; and then she would act the like sport herselfe with her stallions. One of her great Gallants was Crooke-back't Cecill, Earl of Salisbury. John Aubrey

The longed for, leaping season of Spring
is upon us: it is time my lord,
your worship, your grace.
Gird your loins, prepare to saddle up.
Ladies, take your usual place.
But first we'll limber, conga eel
through all with-drawing rooms,
filly and colt alternate. Proceed,
step you lightly with forearms clasped about
each forward haunch. Parade gaily
before my gilded mirrors -
I will have my dainty dressage.
Pull back the curtains, let May's rich sunshine
flood the room, disperse all crafty shadows.
I'll have no aristocratic diffidence.
Slap. Come, measure your filly,
hand over hand. Let the first colt
test my hind quarters and say
if he will out-distance me.
Align yourselves, stand at the ready
but observe the order of rank. Salisbury,
you're fourth, but hump it as you may.
Now, Sirs,
bridle me fast, for we must ride,
ride all the way home and come at last
with flying tackle to Banbury Cross.

1577

Matthew Godwin

He kneels before
an organ, not an altar
prays to the god whose music
conducts his life

Curls follow curves
in the fluting of his ruff
his Oxonian gown crimsons
over black sleeves and shoes

Around him scent
of flowers, fruit, wheat-sheaves
trees' leafing architraves
voices of women

*

He lifts his hands
the choristers draw breath
before he takes them up
into his heaven

1586

Zeal-of-the-Land Busy

> *to feed the vanity of the eye or the lust of the palate, it were not well,*
> *it were not fit, it were abominable, and not good.*

There's the milkmaid again, I see her throughly -
a shame on her froward ways - surely she
does not need to touch the teats quite so barely,
are there no gloves made for the purpose?
I'll search the scriptures, Oh the Word!
the Lord be praised!
                                What a land
of perdition this has become -
not content with fairs and booths,
so full of sinful trickery
and gulling, we now have theatres!
There's that awful Shitspeare strutting about,
an actor-manager he calls himself....
well! but praise be to Zion, it is likely
the Lord shall slap the plague about
and theatres will be closed this summer.
Ah, the Lord takes vengeance on all their sin:
they shall burn in hell for eternity.
How kind is the Lord, so full of mercy
and justice! How I thank my God
that I am chosen, one of the Elect.
Tomorrow is the Sabbath Day when we
shall break bread at the Lord's table; how well
I know there are those who dress in vestments still,
mutter from a missal at their altars
and dabble in all kinds of popish devilry.
The day shall come, the day of reckoning
when they shall have to answer for their crimes:
they will all be taken from hence and hanged.
Mark my word, the Lord, he shall not stomach
Antichrist for long, he will not abide
their hateful mass (how loath I am even
to utter that word) without striking them down!
They that have turned away from scripture's Truth
are all destined for perdition .
How wonderful is the Lord, Oh his name
be praised for ever.
                       To thy tents O Israel!

c.1600

The Inventory of Edward Cookes

A true Inventorie of all the goods, cattell and chattells of
Edward Cookes, late of Cobley in the county of Warwick,
Esquire, deceased, taken and prised the eighteenth day
of June in the seaventh yeare of the raigne of our Soveraigne
Lord Charles...

Imprimis.   His weareing apparrell with the appurtenances, ú30.

Item.   money in his purse, ú10.
            in the greate parloure one table, one chayre, six joynde
            stooles, three carpitts, one Lute, sixe cushens, one
            Sitterne, and one payre of tables.

Item.   Bookes in his Studdy, ú5.
   In the Pantry, Pewter of all Kyndes.
   In the Kitchen, Brase of all Kynds.
For brewing, Hoggsheads, barrels and payles.
For the hemp and Flax, spynning wheeles and
other Implements of Husewrie.

In the greate Chamber one trundle bedd, two
ffether bedds, one wool bedd, one cradle.

Lullay, lullay, thou little tiny...
But he died without issue.

In the Gallerie, one beddstead and oates in the
fflowre.

No rocking the cradle.
no lulling with the lute.

Marie's arms aching empty.
Silent the futureless hall.

One payre of tables in the parloure
for no more backgammon evenings.

She walked in the gallery after he'd gone.
Up and down, up and down. Down.
Plagued with her memories
Ring o' ring o' roses
A pocket full of posies
Atishoo atishoo
We all fall down   *1620*

Civil Disorder

               i

A zig-zag, criss-crossing of landscape,
horses hard driven and the tilled
and tilted fields hacked and turned
into a grid of theological tract -
sweat from the flanks, steam from flared nostrils -
all is purpose without distraction,
God's ardour electric in the air...

        possessors of the Truth:
        now they are nameless and unremembered,
        folded away among dry pages.

Boys lead the line with drum and pipe,
gunsmoke obscures a crumpled farmhouse...
and their mouths lie open under gauze,
exude a moth-filled silence.
Leather and iron:
how they were once well strapped, well caged,
barred against all moral perversion!

        now nameless and unremembered...
        lost in a fevered turmoil of spirit.

              ii

Their sugared madrigals turned suddenly sour:

a gentleman's war if ever
war can be so conjoined with gentle.
The boy is questioned again:
Which way? were the horses cold?
how far would *you* say?
Clad in the puffy silks of a ter Borch
and raised on a cushioned stool
he stands, flaxen and curled, the eyes
frightened but arrogant still.

Tensions of silence grip the room
as evening shadows lengthen
across panelled walls, darken
the boy's clouded face

        and all their sugared madrigals
        turned suddenly sour.

Surrender of Oxford, 1646

Feeding the Siege

   Frost paints our windows
but its flowers don't stay.
     What stays with me is fear.

   I carry food to the castle
an hour's walk at night
     when each sound hits my heart.

   Fox and badger know me,
shadows across the path
     glide, slide on black ice.

   At ebbtide I cross the sand.
Moonless the keep rears dark
     as I climb and tap light as a crab.

   My mother comes pale under siege,
from laundering for the men.
     She kisses the bag, my brow

   then finger on lip backs in.
The closed door. Darker dark.
     Out on the long ridgeway

   firstlight pushes my back
coldly light-fingered.
     Outlined on the dead treetop

   a buzzard eyes me.
I softwalk on verges
     creep into the house.

   Dream of flying to peace
and wake to cannonballs'
     crackswishing on the castle.

1646

Brixham Redlanding

The king ordered us back to harbour.
600 horses stayed deep,
some still living were wrecks.
At Helvetsluys they'd sniffed the air. Snorted.
Clear weather, calm. But they knew.
Needed slapping up the gangway.
And it blew, the ships were leaves
on the bumpy seaground. Swept silly.

When the storm abated we set sail again.
5 November. King William lands at Brixham.
Horses stagger on moving ground,
men fall about, dizzied thosts,
their only enemy the weather.

Sergeants and officers searched out billets.
Too few. So they commandeered a field.
A battlefield of red mud, earth's
rich blood streamed over and under our legs,
soft-mattressed, our heads and backs sank in clay
as we slept sweetly in our campagne coats.
Cold as I was I loved that rich red land,
my livelihood and wealth for future years.

1688

View from the Coffee House

This, Sir, is my coffee house,
a refuge from the malodorous street.
You see? Brightly lit and commodious
with nothing of the ale house about it;

Barbarians have been thronging the gate,
poker faced puritans spreading their gloom!
But at last they are silenced, their day is done;
no more do we have to stomach hearing
how plagues and fires are engines of God's wrath.
Oh let them go to the Americas,
let them preach and quake before the Redskin!

Just mark the bearing of my customers -
a fresh, if mannered stance declares *this* beau
a learned gentleman. With three inch heels
and full length wig he is the very height
of fashion (though stinking like a polecat),
come hot foot panting from the Chapel Royal.
Above all, he is our man for music.
Who can understand his discourse?
Apparently quite a number, for they
flock here to take their coffee, all nodding
and wagging their knowing heads, giving full
and solemn face to each word he utters.

Names? Well, there's Mr Purcell, just mentioned,
and Mr Dryden likes to step this way -
you note the sort that patronise my house!
You observe: my house is now a market,
pointing to the frequent signing of papers.
Most likely, for with this new ensurance
a man's goods can be left on the sea bed
- whole cargoes can be lost - and still payment
is made. It's beyond my understanding!
No matter. We are pleased to serve coffee,
producing aromatic aid to talk
and the passing of documents -
and all most legally carried forward!

1690

Witchcrazed

It began with my Curiosities.
Shining stones, a man-shaped twig,
a toadskin and a fish-eye.

The little girls hung at my gate
hopped like scared birds,
eyes round beads of jet, glittered.

One way to get company.
I asked them in and showed my store:
such things as my daughter played with.

They came again, often. Made up tales,
screamed, saw creatures, spoke magic -
did I say that word? There was no harm.

One day the justice came with his men.
They turned out every drawer and corner,
threw my treasure in a writhing sack.

They could tell tales! Dark imaginings
I never could draw out of my green dreams,
my small lore and love of growing things.

I could not understand the judge's words,
only the pain of what they did
day after day, with ratstraw at night.

I welcome the orange fire. And know
hell is not burning brand, but what
humans breed out of maggotbrains.

1710

Hogarth's Progress

When he turns to paint
to engrave with a brush

he changes his self-portrait
rubs out chisel and gravers

sets art above craft
the subtler means of hair

to brush feature and skin
hands that know hard work

or Mistress Garrick's white ones
firm as she seizes the actor's pen.

The quirk of a grog blossom
and above all eyes that light on us

looking at them. Then
the gloss of silks, each fold

as alive as its wearer
in laces, gowns, waistcoat design

nose-set, lip-curl, line
of eyebrow and ear. The tale

of a baby fed with cherries
above him a small Time with scythe

and close by a cat savagely set
on murdering a cagebird.

Cherry and bird and child
their beautiful lifeblood runs
under the glare of the end.

1750

Pleasure Box

Foxes went to the shore rocks
looking for stranded fish
to take back to the earth.
Badgers built setts in the woods
and birds marked out territories.
Then, undergrowth scythed
ground levelled, foundations laid
a man saw the villa in his head.
A view from each window
that called in the eyes
of sun and moon. Heard
the sea's voice accompany
strings in the music room
and silks' swish, soft silver sounds.
A laugh, low, a sigh, a groan.

He drew out walks, steps, bowers
and all the offices. Arranged
for good summers and
a crisping of frost to whet
guests' Christmases. Yes,
he had chosen the perfect site
for his years of grace. The wild
residents withdrew and left their dens
to dogs. They'd be back one day.

And the builder died, as so often
men do who erect stones
against their passing. Stones and foxes
hold the secrets of the land.

1764

The King, the Poet and the Whore
After Karen Blixen's tale, 'Converse at night in Copenhagen'

I saw him before the Poet did
as he entered soaked to the skin
through velvet, silk and heavy cloak.
Knew him. Not that I'd seen him before.
But his eyes and his hands
spoke for him: king on the tiles
run from warders, wife, mistress.
Up to the heights where I rule,
if they only knew that.

Then we both greeted him, Poet and I.
I'd wept, earlier. In this attic
I've been downed to the basement
if not buried, often. So I had wept.
Then when I looked at his eyes that saw,
under the royal rage he had promised himself,
what waited on him - a cage to live in,
free only out of his mind - this last flight
like the lark, singing with gin,
divinely royal - ah, I was glad
to share my heights. Then my Poet,
ruler of words finer than palaces and pundits,
of the gin bottle and the heavens,
blessed the two of us
and left for ground level.

I roast apples for them on my stove
and give them my wealth of freedom,
dry their tears as they shed themselves
over and over and over again.
My kingdom has room for every sad man.

1767

The Age of Reason

A library of silences gathers round
the solitary figure hunched over
a spread volume. Words; by definition
this gruff lexicographer has become
their master: 'Dictionary Johnson', now settled
in late middle age to recognition
and recompense. But caution is needed
in approach, some trepidation even,
for he is continually under
the *'baleful influence of an horrible
hypochondria'*. Softly, George III
advances: *'Sir, here is the king'*. Johnson starts,
gesticulates involuntarily
in the Garrick manner (*'who's for Poonsh?'*).
Was he fond of going thither to Oxford?
(Johnson sees a pair of shoes left outside
his door at Pembroke now 40 years back -
his face colouring with humiliation)
- Yes, sometimes, but always glad to return.
Was he writing anything?
-No, he had pretty well told the world
all he knew, had done his part as a writer.
*'I should have thought so too if you had not
written so well.'* Johnson falls silent:
'It was decisive' he declared later,
not wishing *'to bandy civilities
with my sovereign'*.
                        The odour of polish
and rich bindings fills the companionable
silence as the two men face each other,
one middle aged, lonely, melancholic
and the other eccentric and remote.

The king recalls and contrasts the antics
of other "great men", remembering the outburst
of Clive when pressed under investigation:
*'By God, Mr Chairman, at this moment
I stand amazed at my own moderation'*.
Bullies. 'Now then, India... where was that? What?'

Both were satisfied but time was not kind:
twenty years later the king dismounted
from his carriage in Windsor Great Park

and addressed an oak as the King of Prussia.   *1767*

**William Cowper leaves John Newton's house and returns to Orchard Side.
Olney, May 1774**

        i

Newton could well ponder: Heaven help us
if Mr Cowper gets the shakes again;
even the prospect of children away
at school gives him a fit of the trembles.
Mrs Unwin - his own 'Mary' - must watch
that his affections don't get out of hand!

What could have possessed the woman to let
him believe that there should be a union
between them to placate his troubled breast
over a question of propriety?
No wonder it caused his melancholy
to rise from the gloomy depths of his mind.

A benign confinement: each day's routine
reduced to a square of blank effacement,
a regime of retirement for Cowper -
nothing must come near him that could excite.
Afternoon tea with Puss, Tiny and Bess
(his three tame hares) would be more than enough.

That William Cowper - so gentle a man -
should seek to take his own life! Deadliest
of sins coming from one of God's elect.
Yet better now, *and* writing hymns of praise
which must surely calm his turbulent soul,
return him to the bosom of the Lord.

ii
Newton could well ponder: a lingering smell
of death still hung about him like a bloom
of fetid air. Manacles and shackles
could cause the flesh to rot, fall away
from the bone, greening. It took just a quick
nod of agreement over the body

to decide - then followed a single blow
and chute overboard. It was the smell,
of course, that told you first, rising even
through the stench of the hold. Corpse after corpse,
he witnessed the serried ranks of death
and each night their faces still rose like moons.

Newton, who through grace had now seen the light,
escaped the press gang only to return
as slaver, dealer in human flesh,
rising eventually to shipmaster,
flying all colours on his way to hell,
until a conversion that rivalled St Paul's:

and the good Lord had brought him to Olney
to stir the hearts of these simpering folk,
where they attend cucumbers and melons,
keep songbirds in cages and cultivate
Sensibility. He'd evangelise
them all, *and* tend to Cowper's black demons.

1774

John Cookes of Kennington walks to his City Office

A fine morning; it brings out the crowds
Buy my 4 Ropes of hard Onions

How they surge to Tyburn this Hanging Day
Pretty Maids Pretty Pinns Pretty Women

My walk is shorter over new Blackfriars Bridge
Twelve pence a peck Oysters

So many paupers still flocking to Town
Fair Lemons and Oranges

Must get a man to paint my good house
Fine Writing Inke

A right choice to live in
Kennington Lane
Any work for John Cooper

Of all the new districts it suits me best
Knives or Cisers to grinde

And remember the silk bales for my wife
Old Satin Old Taffety or Velvet

And buy the News for Pitt's speech
Crab Crab any Crabs

Send the boy for my broidered weskit
4 Paire for a Shilling Holland Socks

Tonight the Alderman comes to dine.
I must home early to decant the wine.

Lilly White Vinegard three pence a Quart!

(Acknowledgments to P. Tempest, Cryes of London, 1711)

1780

After the Stirling Ranges, the Karri Forests, Western Australia

James Stirling stood here
  two centuries back
looking over the breasted hills
  wondering

how his boots could tread the bush
  into submission,
thorn, snake, iron-trunked grass-tree,
  deadly spider.

Haloed with insistent flies
  and merciless sun
fell on his knees before
  the gold blaze of a Christmas tree

Christ never knew
  and pushed on down
into the incomprehensible shade
  of tall straight karri trees.

1827

From the Unpublished Diary of Syms Covington

This is my private one; I keep it
after I've written out Don Carlos's notes
back on board The Beagle with his finds

in the amazing world of South America.
I feel his passion even when I'm laden
with Megatherium and Mastodon bones.

My deaf ear dulls our murder of weird live creatures
though I wonder sometimes if we are justified.
There's pain enough among us, God knows.

Darwin's discoveries change our lives as we
eat these beasts and fruits with strange shapes
and tastes, poison or paradise fare?

He pushes back time and we goggle
at views so long the prophets fall
from their summits into unfathomable valleys

while I set down millennia in my round hand
as lucid, limpid and curved as any river
that irrigates the geology of a land.

1833

The Engineer

Houdini-like he has escaped
from the inhuman chain mail curtain
that forms his backdrop. Having wriggled free
he stands nonchalantly smoking a cigar
and fully clad in his stove pipe hat
set at a saucy angle to the world.
Isambard Kingdom Brunel: bridge builder
with the mellifluous name.
                           But less adept
at engineering a children's game:
he once played the old trick
of making a penny vanish
but it went wrong
and he swallowed the coin and turned blue
when some quick-thinking man
had him turned upside down
and they whacked his back
until he coughed out the penny
which certainly saved his life.

Now, crossing the Tamar into Cornwall
the bridge proudly announces BRUNEL
- and who else? - we might ask
as the train lifts high into blue air
amid gulls winging in from Plymouth Sound.

c.1850

A Victorian Christmas Card

Snow fills the trenches quickly,
sweeps into sensuous folds
and lit by flares
streaks green in night's soft hollows;

ice needles glance along the wind,
each a prism
splintering the white light of dawn
into spectra of lurid colour.

At Scutari
lantern lights throw silhouettes
of women, bending.

Crimea - winter 1854/5

Little Wife

He was already laid out
like a corpse before he died;
'gastric fever' is what
they said but all knew

that meant typhoid.
His fretful breathing
could be heard in the next room.
Distraught, she rushed in

towards the bed:
'Here is your little wife'
she murmured in German
and bent to kiss the cold face.

The medical men were brusque,
would brush her aside
as a confounded nuisance
with no business to be there

but she was already close
bending over the dead Albert.
'Now there is no-one left
to call me Victoria' she wailed.

1861

Brothers

I

The Home Landowner

His stay-at-home feet
  are planted in good mud
his horse splashes through after
    the small red fox.
He reads about his brother's itched feet
around and down under
    as he downs his claret
    in the northern dark.

Dreams of jungles, spears
  and conquests
of treasure in flesh and mine
    but settles for closer wars and
  long evenings
land even if wet rather than
    sea or sky.
Devotes his liver to wine
    rather than whisky
and keeps his peasants down
    with poverty and law.
His wife plans marriages
    and settlements.

Over his sundowner
   the brother muses on whether
    black is as black
as white soiled at the edges
  mist slinks round
that 200 years on
    whites out the land.

II

The Colonist

Itch in the mind
that wildfired to the feet
and set him off from
small green shires
to paint the world pink
keep the sun busy.

Grand apartments
stand cold
the bountiful lady
has left the village
to its draughts and coughs
and gone to tend darker eyes
before malaria gets her.

Small at first
 a clearing near the landing place
modest fires and not much ash.
Clashes enough and people to subdue
with power, powder and shot.

Cradle by the fire
your sleeper had a scream
turned to a bellow
and white was dirty
brought coal-burning engines
new kinds of death
silenced 500 Aboriginal tongues
and took its fill.

Up here now at 40,000 feet
the sun never relents
outshines all other light
that apes it. Today
there's no pink and green
in the world below
we have laid fuses
and set a forest fire
big enough to blind
the Indian and Pacific Oceans.

1890

1915

He marched down the lane to me at evening
one of those days that doesn't want to end
and the sky is a luminosity that sends
off shadows, holds up dark from falling.

He stopped as if to attention, seeming
on parade, a soldier drilled not to bend
but suddenly at ease put out a hand
to brush my forehead, lightly, loving.

'Your face is the lantern I shall take with me
into the loud gloom we're making for,
with the red sinking into war,
turning your tears to blood endlessly.'

He pulled me roughly into the wood, my breath
crushed out of me by the uniform of death.

Sepia

walking into my family cemetery
here they all are
staring out from pieces of card
into a future
that will resemble the past
with everything safe in God's hands -
a mud-filled trench was still something
at the end of the garden
or the field's edge

overdressed to the point of suffocation
you couldn't unbutton that lot
in a hurry but then
one did not wish to be at all unseemly

'Grandmother Elizabeth Argent'
my great-grandmother silver haired
with a slightly twisted lower lip
eyes bright with benignancy
obviously kindly
obviously dead

and a great-great-grandmother Page
coming into the frame
fiercely at an angle
but distantly
is she behind glass?
she's certainly making her point
with her elaborate black silk bow
almost garrotting her
but we can't hear
maybe we're deaf
they were blind
that's for sure
but who can blame them?
it was clearly a man's world
although *some had still to make their way*

this young man's for India

how proudly they sit or stand
in large family groups
pre-Somme pre-Freud pre-Durex
pre-everything
with their insecurities swept and kept
under the carpet   *1902/1909*

Peacock House

The peacock house by the moorgate
weeps from lowered eaves
as mist drizzles out the view.

Slant pseud-Tudor timbers
spell the 20s. Good days
with holidays for rounders families,

when plimsolls' whited sepulchres
sat out dry nights on windowsills
dreaming of candlelit charades,

or Murder to giggled accompaniment.
Old days. Now the debonair daughter
sits in the folds of her face.

They curtain her profile. Her eyes,
bone nose and fingernails sense
the grip of the brooding moor

its ancient ageless stories
balms and blizzards. She knows them.
Inside, her books rot as mice celebrate

while a peacock patrols her roof
as she sits between heaven and earth,
crone at millennium's end.

1926

1943
On the flight over I was a child
thinking of toys: make-up and clothes
whether I'd remembered to pack those
essentials, barring my mind to wild

grief for the hands and faces left behind.
Dropped out of safe darkness and met
by hands hardened to risk, I was set
in the teeth of the wind.

Hidden, I made ready the transmitter.
My life coded explosive words
from shadows with ghost names heard
in a keytap, cocksnooping death, sweetbitter.

Now in this adult cell of pain I croak singing
'I have nothing to say, nothing to say, nothing...'

1990

Sand. Khaki, colour of dust.
My permanent make-up, well worn.
Blue only hinted at by dawn
before heat bakes a crust

over skin, eyes, vehicles, food
and both sides send purple death
faster, further through distant breath
with only aim, no colour, no good.

Along the killing road black and brown
of murdered metal. A human statue
plinthed on a tank. His black hue
burns eyes the world round.

And stays and stays, a scar no flood
can wash clean, stubborn as blood.

William's Century

       i

William, 94, a large man,
tall and full of vigour,
a head of thick black hair,
looks fit but had stomach ulcers
which are healed now

elegant in his red and black dressing gown
'going home on Monday' he's pleased to say

the catholic priest stops to say hello
then passes on
'I'm a catholic' says William

- Signed up for the army with a friend
both 15 but said they were 18
and were accepted there and then

Ypres 1917: the ruined Grande Place
toothed against the skyline
and William delivering dispatches
to the Canadians,
crossing in the open...
the Canadians filtering back
to shoot the Germans in their dugouts ...

      ii

and after this, still in service,
sent to Dublin then on to Cork:

Michael Collins - 'a murderer' -
at the Post Office Easter 1916;
Connolly wounded and executed
while strapped to an armchair;
de Valera - against the Treaty - *not* Irish
but born in New York, father a Spaniard

the Irish army split in two
and William in a gun battle with the IRA
lasting one and three quarter hours
(here he mimes a shouldered rifle, firing
imaginary bullets into the ward)

      iii
then with the Royal Artillery Company
in World War II
attempting to block German subs
using concrete slabs and high explosives -
an attempt which failed -
and taken prisoner to Poland
where he was finally released by the Russians
'no wonder the Germans lost' he says
'the Russians were strong, marching with their accordions,
and many Mongolians on horseback ...'

released
        then sent to Belsen to 'help clear up'
(he falls silent, starts to weep at this point)
by now commissioned and made a captain:
the sergeant said 'What do you think?'
William: 'I don't know what to think'

opened a room - full of children's shoes -
all the children gone
but an overpowering smell of urine
the ovens discovered ...
'five million, five million Jews in Poland
before the war' he shouts
'now there are twenty thousand'

      iv
British National Party visited recently
and William asked 'What about the five million
Jews who were murdered ...?'

- 'Why, did you count them?
It's all Jewish propaganda'

reverts to World War I -
women giving white roses and feathers
to men in civilian clothes,
ensuing street fights, community unrest

and the regimental mascot dog,
killed by shrapnel and buried
in canvas alongside soldiers ...

1997

1997
   - Contrasts & Consolations

For the casualties of war, the insistent babies
For the starving, gluts of international food
For the lonely, the sparkstruck love of families
And for the cancer and Aids-felled, the long-lived

For the child widow, the golden wedded
For the murdered girl, the lovers' weal
For the failed artist, the armless who succeeded
And for the blind, the brilliance of Braille

For the bulldozed tree, the rescued garden
For the fouled sea, the cleansed ocean
For the caged creatures, the return to freedom
And for the carers, gratitude's devotion

For the black silence of death, the music of wordshapes
And for the blare of cities, illimitable landscapes.

At Life
2000 A.D.

All is green in the dusk of the station.
I am back from the city weather,
its clouds of skin and bone
raining showers of thought,
its fat cats greased with gold
and lean birds blue with cold.

Trees give me breath for the road
to drive alone, released
from the crushed and poisoned queue,
to curve corners, rise and fall
slung by the gale, peppered by hail,
rocked by the boat of the moon.

I'll be back in the city, anon,
hammering out some meanings,
tube-riding with unknown shades
whose black and blue china eyes
can turn green if challenged with smile
or white with murderous scowl.

I'll hear songs in the tunnel's draught
against screams of the torn-apart child,
know virtue engendered by grief
for the death of a dicing princess,
research the long story of words
in the seconds the century holds.

NOTES

1   1AD. The young woman is a Celt, living in the West Country in a period of peace.

2   1AD. 'Nature's bonfire burns on': Gerard Manley Hopkins (1844-89), 'That Nature is a Heraclitean Fire'.

5   750. Another Celtic girl from the Iron Age, but now the Saxons are sweeping through southern England taking the Celtic farms and lands. Even when they do not kill the occupants, they use them as slaves.

7   850. From this time on, Scandinavian raids were frequent along the east and south coasts, and the resident Saxons suffered. Here it is imagined the Saxon girl is willing to be taken into the Viking camp in a secluded bay.

8   700/900. i) The term 'Bretwalda' probably means Ruler of Britain, of which Christopher Brooke, in *The Saxon and Norman Kings* (William Collins, 1963), says, 'perhaps we should not take this too seriously; it was apparently copied shortly after King Athelstan's death...'
991. ii) The Battle of Maldon, Essex, in which Bryhtnoth, Ealdorman of Essex, was killed. Bryhtnoth was a benefactor of Ely and is buried beneath the cathedral.

9   1068. Gytha was the Danish wife of Earl Godwin, whom she married about 1020, and mother of King Harold, 1022-66. She held various estates in Devon, including Exeter and the South Devon village of Sherford, as well as in other counties. Traces of Norman architecture remain at Sherford church.

10   1069. Danish raiders harried South Devon during the 11th and 12th centuries. This event is recorded for the parish of Thurlestone in the responses to Dean Jeremiah Milles's questionnaire to parishes, c. 1755:
' Tis said that the Danes having ... killed the husbands in order to gain their wives for themselves, these brave women had a secret watchword concerning "roosticocks, so well communicated to each other, that the same night every bloody ravisher was sacrificed in revenge..." '

11   1086. After the Conquest William (1035-87), divided England among his knights, giving them fairly small estates remote from each other in order to prevent the rise of possible rivals with great landholdings. In Devon, William of Falaise was such a Norman; his neighbour Judhel built Totnes Castle, a moat and bailey still dominating the town from its rise at the top of the steep main street. Beornwynn had been the Saxon owner of Dartington Hall and its lands in the 8th century.

12   1098. An imaginary re-creation of the building of Durham Cathedral. A sheila-na-gig was a female fertility symbol, often with legs wide open. The phrase 'slow, solemn rhythms' is from Alec Clifton-Taylor, *The Cathedrals of England*, Thames and Hudson, London 1967.

13   1199. Richard 1, Coeur de Lion, (1157-99), died trying to defend his Angevin inheritance, gallant if unpractical to the last.

14   1203. Eleanor of Aquitaine (1122?-1204) was married to the vacillating Henry II, 1133-89.

15   1238. Accounts of eyres, courts of itinerant justices in the late 12th and the 13th centuries, give details of many such incidents.

16   1250. Oxford University, a group of independently run colleges, arose out of monastic foundations established before 1200 by monks belonging to the orders of Dominicans, Franciscans, Benedictines and Cistercians. Stanza four refers to a later institution, The Bodleian Library, founded in 1602 by Sir Thomas Bodley (1545-1613).

17   1349. The Black Death harrowed England and the rest of Europe from 1348 onwards.

19   1448. Almost a found poem, with much material taken from *The Pastons, a family in the Wars of the Roses*, edited by Richard Barber, The Folio Society, London 1981. The Pastons were a well-to-do family living in Norfolk in the 15th century.

20   1453. All three men named in the dedicatory epigraph were composers: Walter Frye (d.1474/75?) and John Dunstable (c.1390-1453) were English; Johannes Ockeghem (c. 1420 -c.1495) was from the Low Countries.

21   1471. Lambert Simnel (1487-1525), son of an Oxford joiner (some say a pastrycook) was persuaded by a priest, Richard Symonds, to claim himself the nephew of Edward IV, 1442-83. He was crowned in Dublin as Edward VI, gathered enough supporters to attempt an invasion of England in 1487, but was defeated. Henry VII recognised that Lambert had been duped and ordered him to work as a scullion in the royal kitchens, later promoting him to falconer.

22   1471. Robert Whitingham, faithful counsellor and attendant to Queen Margaret of Anjou (1430-82), who escaped from prison to rejoin her before the fateful Battle of Tewkesbury when her husband Henry VI (1421-71), of the Red Rose, the Lancastrians, was defeated by Edward (1442-83), leader of the White Rose Yorkists, who became Edward IV. Margaret took part in battles herself, earning the name of she-wolf or tigress. Owlpen Manor in Gloucestershire lies to the south of the River Severn. Its 'Hall Chamber' above the Great Hall is traditionally associated with Queen Margaret. Here she spent the night before the battle, in which her only son died and the Lancastrian cause was lost.

24   1483. It was well known that Richard III (1452-85) used his lavatorial sessions to make plans. Sir James Tyrell was said to have been ordered by Richard, when Duke of Gloucester and anxious to seize the crown, to see to the killing of his two young nephews, the twelve year old Edward V and his younger brother, in the Tower of London. Richard died on Bosworth Field in 1485, Tyrell was executed 19 years later. Richard's emblem was a white boar.

26   1487. The hound is in Kings College Chapel, Cambridge.

27   1497. Perkin Warbeck (1474-99) was an impostor to the throne from 1491 to 1497, posing as the younger of the murdered sons of Edward IV.

28   1525. William Tyndale (c.1494-1536), translator of the New Testament and half of the Old from the original Greek and Hebrew into English for the first time. The phrases in italics are Tyndale's own. If some of them sound very familiar, that illustrates the power of his language. Tyndale was strangled and burned outside Brussels.

31   In 1545, two years before his death, Henry VIII (1491-1547) was at Portsmouth to see his new warship Mary Rose sail out to defend the land against the French. Suddenly she listed and sank within minutes, drowning most of her crew. A large part of the hull was raised in the 1980's and a remarkable quantity of objects and artefacts saved for exhibition and conservation.

32   1577. The quote is from Aubrey's *Brief Lives*, c. 1680 (the Oliver Lawson Dick edition, Martin Secker & Warburg, 1949).

33   1586. Matthew Godwin's memorial, given by 'G. M.', is on the north wall of the nave of Exeter Cathedral. A bachelor of music from Oxford, and master of music at Canterbury and Exeter, he died on 12 January 1586 at the age of 17 years 5 months.

34   c. 1600. A character in Ben Jonson's *Bartholomew Fair*, 1631.

35   1620. Unlike much of the material of these poems, the inventory here is based on an actual one.

37   1646. Fort Charles, Salcombe, South Devon, is said to have been the last Royalist stronghold in Devon to hold out against the Parliamentarians. It was strengthened by the building of an outer layer on to Henry VI's drum keep by Captain Edward Fortescue, who with 66 men and two laundresses, ten other officers and a chaplain, was governor of the castle until articles of surrender were signed on 7 May, 1646, when, with other conditions, the defenders were permitted 'free liberty to march to Fallowpit (Sir Edmund's residence some 7 miles away) with there usuall armes, drums beatinge and collers flyinge...'

38　1688. William of Orange (1650-1702), landed at Brixham in November 1688, to no resistance from the populace. The day, the 5th, was not one of bonfires but of drenching rain, which many of the men remembered, though some returned to settle there.

40　1710. Although witch hunting did not reach the pitch of hysteria that occurred in the Pyrenees and northern Spain in the 17th century, there were numerous cases of witch burning in Britain, at its height between 1550 and 1650. Persecution of 'witches' continued, and the last burning recorded, in Devon, took place as late as 1782. This witch is invented, as a typical example.

41　1750. William Hogarth (1697-1764), painter and caricaturist.

42　1764. The holiday taken in Britain began to be a social custom in the late 18th century. Even before that, landowners had started to build villas or summer residences beside the sea or in beautiful settings. The Moult at Salcombe was begun by John Hawkins, of the seafaring family, in 1764. The term 'Pleasure box' was concurrent with 'Shooting Box' or 'Lodge'.

43　1767. Based on a story by Karen Blixen (1885-1962). 'Converse at Night in Copenhagen,' is set in the 18th century, in which two of the characters are the king of Denmark and the poet Johannes Ewald (1743-81).

44　1767. The incident described in the poem is from Boswell's *Life of Doctor Johnson* (1791). J H Plumb puts Robert Clive's situation regarding his antics in India rather nicely in *England in the Eighteenth Century*, Pelican Books 1950: The Commons brought themselves to investigate Clive's actions, but they were satisfied with his outburst: 'By God, Mr Chairman, at this moment I stand amazed at my own moderation'.

45　1774. The poet William Cowper (1731-1800) suffered a mental breakdown after which he stayed with John Newton, Calvinist hymn writer and former slaver.

46　1780. Many wealthy residents of London lived on the South Bank during this period, and would have walked to their city offices if they did not travel by boat.

47　1827. Sir James Stirling founded what was to become the state capital of Western Australia, Perth.

48　1833. Syms Covington was a naturalist who travelled with Charles Darwin on his voyages of discovery.

50　1854-55. Scutari, where Florence Nightingale (1820-1910) revolutionised the nursing profession.

51   1861. When Prince Albert was ill, the authorities gave out that he had 'gastric fever'. No one was fooled and all knew it meant typhoid. His doctors tried to keep his wife, Queen Victoria, away from his sickbed.